FREEDOM WARRIOR

by

Gwen Van Velsor

YELLOW ARROW
PUBLISHING
Baltimore, MD

Other books by
Gwen Van Velsor

Follow That Arrow: Notes on Getting Here from There
Prayers for Woodlawn
Vade Mecum

"Freedom's just another word for nothin' left to lose."

Kris Kristofferson

for
Ella Seraphim

What I've Learned About...

MESSENGERS OF HOPE

Despite walking over 500 miles to get to Santiago de Compostela, my pilgrimage does not feel complete when I reach it. It is like arriving at the top of a mountain only to find I had summited the first foothill rather than the peak. My body is weary, my pack heavy, and my questions unanswered. Making my way to the Santiago de Compostela Cathedral, its steps worn smooth with the feet of pilgrims over hundreds of years, I sit in on an English-speaking mass in one of the rear chapels. I am not Catholic, but try my best to follow the kneeling and crossing throughout the service, in order to fit in. It is raining outside and the slick shoes of the parishioners squeak on the stone floor. A statuette of Mary, dressed in brilliant blue, looks down on us, tearful, her empty arms extended. I take the bread and wine offered, hoping a little Holy Spirit will come to my aid.

At the end of the service, a nun in a turtleneck layered under a gray sweatshirt invites the motley congregation of pilgrims and travelers to have coffee at a nearby cafe. I follow her through the massive wooden doors of the cathedral and across a quaint cobblestone street. We make polite conversation over wedges of almond cake and café con leche. When the last of the others excuse themselves to go and it is just me and the nun, she turns to me, knowing that I need to talk.

"Tell me why you have walked the Camino," she says. Her glasses still have a few scattered raindrops around the edges.

I sense no need to mince words. "My husband had an affair. I left home. Needed a change."

"I see," she says without pause. Her accent is faintly Irish. "Will you go back to him?"

"I don't know what to do," I finally say. "I hoped the answer would be clear to me when I made it here. It's not. I don't know what to do."

"Have you asked God?"

I had, in fact, asked God, fervently.

"Yes," I say, looking at my hands. "I really have."

"God is speaking to us all the time, and it's our job to listen," she says with complete confidence, again, no hesitation, no pause.

• • •

It was exactly the message I needed to hear. Some say that seizing opportunity is like dancing on a knife's edge. Not at all. I imagine God sending an army of messengers out to the front lines of my personal journey, mostly to cheer me on, sometimes to provide nourishment, and other times to guide me back to the path when I am lost. I imagine this is true for all of us. He is trying to reach us all the time, constantly trying to communicate through any means necessary what His will is for our lives.

Along my life's journey, I will find friends, enemies, danger, love, beauty, fear, and faith. I will have exciting adventures and those that make me cower in the trenches. I'll walk in cold rain and enjoy endless, sunny vistas. I'll forget myself and find myself, curse humanity and gorge on it. My feet are all that will carry me, and when these wear out, luckily there will be cars and trains and lots of other people willing to take me where I need to go. Some of these willing people are friends or family, while many more are perfect, angelic strangers. I will need these companions as much as I need food and shelter. As I make my way through dark woods or along a peaceful shore, by foot, rail, or car, messengers are all around to point the way.

Maybe such messengers will come to me as animals or appear as fellow humans offering strange, yet timely, advice. And maybe they will sometimes come in the form of magical fairies, an army of angels, or a strange dream. They are always there because the creator of this journey doesn't want me to get lost, doesn't require that I pave a tough path through brambles. As I meander through life, my nose in a book or eyes to the sky predicting the weather, I often miss the urgent warnings or gentle steering of these messengers of hope. This is alright because my messengers will keep trying to get my attention, knowing that it can be hard to see them. It's up to me to notice them. It's up to me to believe.

WISHING

High up on Mt. Hood, Timothy Lake is icy cold and filled with trout. A perfect reflection of the sky appears in the water when the air is still. Our boat, with a multicolored mound of gear strapped strategically in place with bungee cords, makes the crossing to camp. We are far away from the regular campground with paved pathways, tiled bathrooms, and access to fresh water. We go where "real nature people camp" Dad always says. This lake is one of our usual summer vacation spots, where my family camps for a week at a time.

Our tiny fishing boat, a flimsy fiberglass hull with plywood nailed together over the front end, complete with portholes, makes a wheelhouse of sorts for our journey. It's decorated with stenciled images of fish and trees in leftover blue house paint. A homemade, ramshackle treehouse on water crammed with our supplies. Closer to shore, Dad jumps onto the pebbly beach, getting his sneakers soaked through, and starts pulling the boat toward land with a frayed rope. His ill-fitting swim trunks have pockets and a belt, topped with a T-shirt torn at the collar—his summertime uniform.

My mom, brother, and I jump out one by one, bearing crates of dried goods, haphazardly folded tarps, and heavy coolers. The lake bottom is a mix of smooth, egg-sized pebbles and dense, slimy plant material. Our dog duo, Bess and Laramie, swim excitedly from the beach to the boat and back again, making it impossible to tell where your feet will end up. My sister is horrified by all of this and won't come out of the boat until it's dragged closer to shore so she can jump to the beach without hitting the water. School hasn't started yet, and she doesn't want to dirty her annual new shoes. I still wear my torn-up pair from last year, although the right shoe has a hole in the sole, scraping the pad of my foot on the ground when I walk.

I quickly escape into the woods, claiming to look for firewood. The forest floor is covered in a moss made of vibrant yellows and greens. Groups of rhododendrons, some with a few straggling blooms, glom onto skinny evergreens. A clearing just beyond the trees near our campsite beckons to me, where I find a makeshift home beneath the tree. Another family must have just left this natural canopy. A countertop of plywood straddles two trees, making a kitchen of sorts. A clothesline hangs taut and high above the ground. Some flat boulders sit upright like couch cushions in front of a perfect fire ring. A deep hole serves as a toilet pit, complete with a branch nailed to a tree to hang toilet paper. The ground is swept and cleared of any brush. I quickly grab an armful of branches and run to share what I have found.

Back at camp, an argument over bent and missing tent poles broils while my sister shoos away invisible bees. I start to explain about the little shack just past the forest edge while dragging one of the coolers to store in our new kitchen. Dad roars at me to leave the coolers alone and help with the tents instead, a large family-sized one for my parents and brother and a smaller four-man tent for my sister and I. Pillows and sleeping bags clutched tightly in hand, I swallow a burst of anger, hot and heavy. I easily set up the smaller tent with only two poles and zip the door behind me after crawling in. Legs outstretched, I push down hard on my knees, hyperextending them until they hurt. This makes the crying stop. Outside, my sister yells for me to get out. I yell back that I'm changing into a swimsuit, which is a lie because it is already on under my clothes, an early preparation for swimming. I need another minute to stop crying.

I eventually emerge from my tent to card tables unfolded and all backpacks safely stowed. Mom and Dad settle into low beach chairs and start drinking beer. Thickly sliced cheese sandwiches make an easy lunch along with a shared bag of potato chips. I tell them again about the house in the trees just behind the campsite. They say they'll look at it later, unenthused.

It's hot and dusty. I search through the already melting ice in a cooler for a black cherry soda. Dad asks me to get a beer for him. I obey, shaking it furiously with my back turned then sprint for the shore after handing it over. My feet go right into the water after I toss off my shoes. The lake is surrounded by evergreens, underbrush ripe with wild lilies, blackberry bushes, and trillium in the boggy parts. A few fishing boats bob on the lake, and other campers unpack far away on its other side. There must be other kids over there. Tiny minnows swim toward my toes in the shallow water. My younger brother is fishing with a stick nearby. I throw a rock in front of him and say it was a fish jumping. He smiles and stares at the spot, hoping to see it jump again. I throw a few more pebbles until he catches on and begins to cry. The adults shout for me to leave him alone. I circle back to the tent to see what my older sister is doing. She shrieks something about horse-flies while clutching a Walkman, screaming for Mom, who finally gets up out of the low-back camp chair to indulge me.

Mom suggests we make a small fairy boat to send off at dusk. The remainder of the afternoon slips by while I carefully assemble the tiny boat. The hull is a curved piece of (deadly) hemlock bark, the size of two hands, with several large pockmarks for storing a bounty of fairy gifts: a pile of wild straw-berries, a collection of tiny pine cones, several acorn husks, and a gleaming crow feather delicately posi-tioned inside. Miniature bouquets of flowers, tied with long pieces of field grass, add the finishing touch. When Dad calls us to dinner, I hide the pre-cious ship behind a boulder until I can launch it. We eat, balancing paper plates piled with pasta on our knees while Dad regales us once again with stories of his famous spaghetti sauce. The sauce is tangy and beefy, heavy handed with garlic powder. I chug another can of black cherry pop—soda is allowed anytime while camping—and quickly eat. Piled high with thick logs for the damp air headed our way, the fire roars like a train gaining momentum.

After dinner, I collect my delicate boat, light a tea candle in the campfire, and walk alone toward the shore, cupping the flame with one hand. In all my nine years, I've never missed an opportunity to make a wish. Dropping a coin into a mall fountain, blowing dandelion seeds mystically into the late summer air, crossing fingers at the sight of a shooting star, or hoping beyond hope in the power of birthday candles. Usually, I wish for a husband or in the very least a boyfriend. Tonight is different. Taking my shoes off, I take a few steps into the gentle lake. Looking out at the flat, undisturbed water, I slide the unsteady bark boat onto its slick surface. I close my eyes and wish to live in the world of fairies and magic. I wish that this world of beer cans, lonely campsites, and screaming brothers would disappear. I wish for freedom.

The tea candle flickers out as my boat exits the

beach inlet. My eyes fix on the shadow drifting off-shore, waiting, the sound of lapping water filling the universe. The sky, a solid glow of burnt orange, descends over everything here on Earth: the water, the trees, my skin, the very air in my mouth. Maybe this is part of the wish-making magic. The air turns cold after a while. I put my shoes back on and head to the campfire. Night has descended; the lake and forest are barely visible under rapidly appearing stars. Dad hands me a small cup with margarita mix and ice. Usually I love this, but tonight I refuse. Mom gives me a knowing look, her face morphing into a cackle.

"Did the fairies take your boat?" she laughs at me.

She is no longer my mom who believes in fairies, the one who came up with the idea to make the boat. I nod yes, warming my chilled limbs by the fire. She can make fun of me and my fairies, but I know better. Fairyland is just out of reach, hidden behind some kind of invisible veil. Just on the other side is a land of acorn cups and dresses made from leaves, a place where winged creatures dance all night and sleep under blankets made from moss. A place where being two inches tall means no one can see you. The place I long to be.

Later in my tent, dreading the scratchy sensation of dry feet against a soft sleeping bag, I snuggle in with my socks still on, the sound of pops and cracks from the fire marking mountain time. The window of the tent is unzipped to reveal a bright and swirling galaxy and the swoosh of shooting stars crossing the sky. This time, I don't make a wish; I just close my eyes and wait for sleep.

It's light enough to see my hands when I wake the next morning. Dad is already up, stoking the fire. After wriggling out of the sleeping bag, the cold insists I pull a sweatshirt on. Unzipping the tent door to a still quiet scene, I listen to a few birds chirping the sounds of dawn. The lake is gray, the sky a flicker of low light against ever-reaching trees. Dew covers a carpet of wild strawberries in a silver mist. Taking a seat in one of the camp chairs close to the fire, Dad smiles and nods at me, a twinkle in his eyes.

A metal spoon clinks against a shallow pan on the camp stove. After tasting his concoction with an index finger, Dad adds a little more chocolate from the Hershey's can, poked twice on top with an old-fashioned can opener. He passes me a blue enameled mug of milk and chocolate, and I hold the steaming cup close to my nose, scraping the milk skin off the top with one finger. Dad stirs cream and sugar into his coffee and resumes chopping potatoes with a dull knife on a battered, wooden cutting board.

As I nudge a stick into the fire with one toe, the embers come back to life in a pile of ash. The sun's rays begin to light the other side of the lake, first the tops of the evergreens, then one hillside, then the water. Little lapping waves sparkle as they make their way to shore. The first morning light warms my shoulders, and I peel off my sweatshirt. The sun feels wild and hot. And perfect. Placing the remainder of my hot chocolate on a stone near the fire, my legs sprint for the beach. Dad chuckles behind me, but I don't stop until I make it to the water.

The icy lake swallows me, my eyes wide open to take in the underwater scene. Down, down into the green water, grabbing hold of the slimy water plants to pull myself deeper toward the silty floor. Little bits of algae dance with the rippling movements of the lake. I look up at the sun's rays slicing through the water and kick my mermaid tail faster toward the center of the lake. There is no sound, only freedom and joy and aliveness. My hair floats around my face in the beauty of this underwater world of sunken fairy boats in a sea of mushy plants. I rest in the silence for as long as my breath allows. Ascending to the surface, my heart full with this newfound, precious secret, I emerge from fairyland.

Our camp on shore looks small and quiet from the water. No one else has even stirred. A single snake of smoke works its way toward the sky from the campfire, keeping my hot chocolate warm. I slowly emerge from the water, and Dad meets me with a towel and a grin. I smile back, though I'll never tell.

THE UNKNOWN

GRANDMA STANDS AT THE stove stirring her rhubarb pie filling. A dozen or more empty pie shells sit at the ready on the picnic-style kitchen table. Grandma never stops talking; even when she asks you a question, she keeps right on. The rest of the family is outside in the garden or watching TV in the backroom. I am probably the only one willing to stay in the kitchen and listen to her today. Sometimes, I tease her about her dentures or talking incessantly on the phone, and she laughs. Mom is amazed by this; she would never dare tease Grandma. They aren't close in that way. Grandma doesn't tell jokes; she mostly gossips about illness and divorce, presenting endless dissertations on who is doing what. She does listen though, in order to glean all that information. And I like hearing about the varieties of flowers she's planting and the way her mother used to can tomatoes. Together, we fill the shells, put on their crusts, and slide them into the oven, four at a time. The pies are destined for the county fair the next day.

While they bake, I venture into the backyard to check on the bunnies in the hutch. They scramble to the edge of their cage for scratches on their heads and ears, and I long to take the gray one home. The garden blooms with a million flowers, bulbs and peonies, roses and lilacs. An unstable footbridge leads across a tiny stream into high grass where a lone cow—a young steer—watches from behind a fence. I walk to the beginning of the dirt road that leads out of their driveway, past a row of trailer homes in rural Oregon, to stare up at a sizeable hill covered in evergreen trees.

Every suppertime at their house, Grandpa gazes up at that same hill, pointing out a sparkle of light midway up. Perhaps a metal roof reflecting the late afternoon sun or a window catching the light, he says. In either case, there is no road going up that high; my grandparents have driven it many times hunting for the glimmer on the hill.

We sit around the table passing a platter of chicken and dumplings. Little rainbows from a cut crystal hanging in the window dance on the bowls of vinegar coleslaw and homemade bread and butter pickles. Grandma slices the corn from her cob because she can't bite it with her dentures. As we eat, I peer out, again, at the rolling, forested hill beyond. I yearn, sometimes urgently, to investigate the glimmer, but more than that, to know what is just beyond those hills. I need to know what exists just out of reach.

LOSS

A SINGLE TEAR ROLLS down his nose, which he dabs
with an embroidered hanky, little purple flowers
sprinkled on the edge of a transparent white fabric. Lots of pink roses in full bloom surround her
casket. It's early spring. We are under an awning at
the cemetery. My cousin, who is not even related to
her, pulls up in a big white truck and stands next to
me, gripping the place between my collarbone and
shoulder. I don't cry until I see the tear, unexpected,
slide from my grandfather's eyes. My grandmother
was a talent, a force, at once pleasant and difficult to
be around. We all knew this was the end of our family. No more Sunday meals or Easter egg hunts, no
more September birthday party for all the cousins or
nightly phone calls. No more chicken and dumplings
or sweet and sour coleslaw. No more crystal rainbows dancing on our bread.

MERCY

OUR MANY CATS DRANK from a fish bowl on the kitchen counter without harming the fish. They enjoyed a bottomless food bowl and ventured in and out of the house as they pleased. They always had fleas and never went to the vet; we couldn't afford it. Sometimes they peed on a blanket or pillow until we finally got them a litter box.

Peachy moved into our household when she was pregnant. She drifted in as a stray friend to our un-neutered gray and white tomcat, Smoky. Gray, white, brown, and peach made up the unique pattern of Peachy's tortoiseshell fur. A pinky peach nose and lovely peach ears made naming her easy. Her litter of three—one white, one gray, and one tiger-striped—arrived soon after she did. Two of her children stayed to join the pack at our house; the other moved in with neighbors down the street.

Peachy never stuck around much, going off for days at a time. When she was home, she would sit and let me pet her for long periods. I'd whisper little songs, and she'd listen steadily to my twelve-year-old stories. She was my favorite.

Peachy liked to peer down from up high. The top of the old upright piano was her usual spot. One day, I began to notice a seepage coming from her ears, small amounts of yellowish fluid that had a bad smell. The seeping continued for probably months. The top of the piano was splattered with the putrid-smelling fluid from when she would shake her head to clear it out. Picture frames, books, false flowers, and knickknacks all had spots from Peachy's ears. I would stand on the bench, crooning to her, rubbing her head, trying to soothe my sick cat. When she could no longer jump down from her high spot, my father took her outside and smashed her head with a heavy rock. This is how it was with pets in our house. I was glad when her suffering was over.

SEARCHING

An ancient vista spills down the cliffs ahead. The purple glow on marble ruins, mottled here and bright there, begs to be admired. We find some flat rocks to sit on while a sharp wind blows cold over our clothes. I move to another spot nearby, and then another, as if this movement will make the wind stop blowing, as if a different flat rock will feel less cold.

POWERLESSNESS

Most of my friends in Hawai'i are surfers. We spend weekend afternoons, many weekday evenings, and occasional overnight camping trips at the beach, in front of the waves. They paddle out, under the gleaming sun, to the spot where the waves don't break, a calm place where even the biggest waves glide smoothly under their boards. They sit beyond the breakers, dangling their legs in perfect peace. As a set of waves moves in toward shore, some paddle in their direction to catch a crest, swooping up to a bent knee position. This shiny carpet carries them toward shore where they abandon their boards for a moment before paddling back to the calm. This pattern goes on for hours and hours. I sit on the shore, longing to join them, to splash my legs on either side of a board, yearning to feel that zing of catching a wave. I look at them from behind glass, trapped.

Every once in a while, I gather up the courage to push my foam surfboard into the water, when the breakers are as small as possible. Making it past the first set, in a panic, I get tossed about by the tiny waves. What my friends call ankle biters feel like monster jaws, swallowing me whole. The gentle, peaceful ocean I could see from shore is a war zone of foam and swirling undertows, sharp coral, and strong tides, pulling and pushing me away from the calm, still place past the breakers. Just beyond reach are my surfer friends bobbing on their boards, splashing and laughing. I can't reach them or that calm place beyond the breakers no matter how hard I fight and thrash. Exhausted, I always return to shore, dragging my foam board back to the sand.

In the water, I am afraid. I cannot plant my foot on the ground. I have nothing to hold on to but an untrustworthy board that floats in whichever direction the water guides it. I can keep trying to fight the ocean, but I'll never win. The powerful waves roll in from miles and miles away, relentless. Thrashing or standing firm won't stop them from overtaking me. I must learn to let them wash over me, to allow the water through and past me. To stop fighting and patiently paddle. I must learn to enjoy the splashy foam and trust that the still, silent waters will be there when I get there. God is in the ocean waves, and that place of calm just beyond is for me, too. I'm just unsure how to get there.

ENVY

MY UNLOCKED FRONT DOOR eases open with a tap of
the foot, our arms full of decorations for my sister-
in-law's baby shower. Leaving our slippers outside
on the porch, we glide inside, laughing and chatting.
The party will have a star theme, and we are hoping
to make a celestial chandelier. I asked Becca to help
after she'd thrown me a fantastic tea party for my
birthday with all the details perfectly in place. Perfect
details are not exactly my specialty.

My spare living room is filled with direct sun-
light from the many windows looking out onto
the Pacific Ocean about a mile away. Our home is
perched on the side of a mountain, resting on a
very steep hill. A light, tropical breeze flows through
the screens, keeping the house cool without AC.
My house is small, an open kitchen is part of the
living area that really only fits a couch and a small

dining table, but it should be enough space to host a dozen or so ladies for the shower. My dog, a terrier mix named Cruiser, and cat, a gray and white tabby named AbbaZaba, come dashing in when I open the back door, cat first, as always. The dog, a medium-sized wiry-haired mutt, obeys the delicate cat like the queen she is. They both screech to a halt by the kitchen, looking up. I ignore them, assuming it's a fly or a spot of light reflected on the ceiling. They are always finding something to chase.

Becca and I continue to chat as we bring bags in from the car and place them on the kitchen counter. Becca stands out like a Granny Smith in a bushel of Red Delicious. In Hawai'i, no one wears nice clothes, but she does, complete with heels, gobs of jewelry, and too much blush. Everyone loves her. She's spunky and generous, loving and thoughtful. She makes me want to use olde tyme adjectives like 'cheery' and 'swell.' Her perfectly round behind belongs on the stool of a soda fountain, sipping Coca-Cola from a glass bottle with a striped straw.

While opening the fridge to get us some cold water, I startle at a flapping sound. A terrified ring-necked dove sits on top of the highest cupboard, trying his best to hold still while looking right at me.

I jump back, then turn to the dog and cat who are sitting at attention by my feet, still looking up. The tiny kitty door in the back causes more problems than it's worth.

Becca giggles with delight. After scolding the cat for bringing the bird in the house, I try putting her on the kitchen counter so she can jump up and get the bird. But she just jumps down instead, content to simply stare at the bird and make weird clicking noises. The useless cat and excitable dog are exiled to the backyard once again as their presence is probably terrifying the bird more than necessary. We open both front and back doors, turn off the lights, and put faith in the instinct of the bird to fly toward the light. Becca continues chatting as if it's just another day, no problem at all, unwavered. Not so much me. I keep one eye on the bird, flinching and covering my head each time he moves to a different position in the kitchen, sure that he will swoop down toward my eyeballs at any moment. That was why he was staring at me with his beady eyes. My resentment builds even more at the droppings the bird is probably leaving on top of my cabinets.

Becca just moved to Hawai'i last year with her husband. While working at the same school, we became friends immediately. She is my friend, but I also kind of hate her. No one is that happy all the time. When she does get mad or sad, she describes it as getting the "blues." And yet, Becca and I have an unnerving amount in common. We have both traveled quite a lot in our young lives and love swapping stories about Europe and China, Australia, and the American Midwest. We both write a blog, like to cook elaborate meals, dabble in painting watercolors, like to dress girly, and adore hosting parties. She, of course, is much better than me at all of these things. She has superb handwriting, actually finishes craft projects, and makes ridiculous cakes including a stunning croquembouche for her own birthday. She takes time to curl her hair and put on makeup. She will pop a bottle of champagne on a Tuesday and actually sing out loud to any song she knows on the radio. Becca likes music from the flapper era and owns many cocktail dresses. She normally glitters with costume jewelry and has actually eaten caviar. She overdresses for every occasion and always pulls it off. She is vibrancy.

Compared to her, I feel as if I am a lazy, sloppy wannabe who can barely put together a quiche. My idea of a fancy party involves homemade lemonade and some crepe paper. My nicest sundress is frumpy and crumpled next to her sleek, empire waist frock. My eyeliner is shaky, mascara always casting a shadow under my eyes, and every shade of lipstick somehow looks ridiculous. She urges me to wear a little color on my cheeks, which I try with much embarrassment.

I am also on the brink of turning twenty-nine and in the midst of the deepest depression I've ever felt. On my days off from teaching, I eat a slow breakfast and watch Dawson's Creek reruns for most of the day, gazing out at the sparkly ocean below, unable to venture out into the world. Sometimes I work in the garden, tending a patch of proud asparagus and unlikely tomatoes. Other times, I eat a bag of popcorn for lunch and take zillions of photos of produce for my blog. I take the dog for a short walk and make dinner for my husband before going to bed by 9 pm. Loneliness finds me sobbing to sleep almost every night.

Becca is my excuse lately for getting out of the house. We go to the farmers market, make crafts, and mess around with tarot cards. She stays home a lot, too, but somehow, I doubt she could understand the depths of my self-loathing. She is always cheerful and upbeat, which is mostly good for me but sometimes unbearable as I'm sure she can see my darkness through the thin veil of smiles, jokes, and chit chat.

After an hour of cutting stars from sparkly paper, we decide that the bird will not fly out on his own. I grab the broom and try shooing him toward the door. This results in a fair amount of screaming from me as the bird darts from one end of the house to the other, easily out of reach. Becca calmly grabs a box from the recycling bin outside. She quietly places the box over the bird where he is currently perched near the stove. He doesn't move. She gets a cookie sheet from under the oven and gently slides the box along the counter and onto the sheet. The bird quietly goes along with this as well. She then carries the bird, box, and cookie sheet outside into the yard, lifts the box, and steps to the side.

Stunned for a moment, the bird turns a little circle before flying up the mountainside and out of sight.

Becca giggles, delighted. I study her silhouette, exasperated.

HEARTBREAK

THE SKY AND ROCKS are black. Dark clouds shroud the moon and stars in slow moving masses. The only light comes from the cherry of his lit cigarette, glowing brightly every few seconds. Little black waves lap the lava rocks around us in a constant rhythm, against the unnatural beat of the music coming from his cell phone. I lie on a smooth patch of cold lava next to him, timing my breath to each drag of his cigarette. Thoughts poke around sharply in my head, loneliness the overwhelming sentiment.

Later that night, we lie next to each other in our tiny backpacker tent below Kīlauea, an active volcano on the Big Island. Little points of moonlight poke through the mesh, a soft blue glow on his arm, bent and pointed away from me. He falls asleep fast, saying nothing. I stare at the blackness, enveloped by that same old empty feeling that visits me this time every night. Like the fuzzy white screen on the TV when there is no signal, a flurry of thoughts keeps me awake. There are only two pictures on our fridge at home. One of my parents and one of his. The photo of my in-laws is posed. They smile at the camera, his arm around her shoulder. They wear matching jackets and stand very straight. The photo of my parents is spontaneous. They are sitting on a giant swing made of driftwood and old ropes. They are pretending to fall backward, my dad's fluffy hair a spray around his crown and my mom's classic smirk sporting a secret on her lips.

After attempting, in vain, to warm instant coffee on sun heated lava rocks the next morning, we trek to the edge of our campground to swim in a shallow lagoon. We've come here to get away from the outside pressures of jobs and our business, of keeping house and pets. To take a break from our separation. We needed some time to reconnect without any noise. I brought him here, to this sacred place I've hiked to alone before, sure that if he could see me, be together in this place, then we could fix us.

The water is warm in the lagoon even though it is cloudy, and we float in the knee-deep natural pool for most of the afternoon. The sand below is salt and pepper and just beyond the shore, the ocean is wild, wind-whipped, and scary. Occasionally a translucent crab will scurry along the water's edge while I search for shells nearer to shore. On the sand, he picks over a pile of coconuts, shaking each to find one with milk. Shearing the top off with a machete, we share the precious liquid inside.

A little while later, we walk away from our private beach, out toward the spiky a'a lava rocks in search of a freshwater pond to rinse off in. Previous campers have left white coral pieces to mark a path through the sharp and patternless lava. The freshwater pond, coated in gold algae, is far too deep inside a lava tube to reach. Instead, we explore a little path beneath a group of palms at the edge of the beach. It leads to an elaborate campsite, now abandoned, complete with a stone barbecue pit and several cleared tenting areas enclosed by hand-built rock walls. A patch of shady trees gives the feeling of a roof. Civilization in the middle of nowhere.

A flurry of sound and movement causes quite a start. An owl, quite close, takes off from an upper branch of a nearby tree toward the top of Kīlauea. I gasp, clutching my chest with one hand and pawing the air for his hand with the other to make sure he sees the same thing. Before we can comment, a second owl zooms off after the first. They fly together for a few seconds, then split off, one up and away toward the mountain, the other low and determined toward the shore.

My heart is still thumping from adrenaline as we walk back to our campsite.

After a dinner of canned chili, I take a bag of M&M's and walk along the shore, alone, to hide my tears and clear my head. I strip off my clothes and lay under the overcast sky, waiting. Finally, he comes looking for me. He just stands next to my bare body, looking out toward the water. I sit up and pull him to sit down while leaning over to kiss him. Instead, he glides a stubbly cheek next to mine, placing a foreign hand on my back. It starts to rain. I slowly wrap myself up in a pareo and walk back to camp, twenty feet in front of him.

An evening of blackness and silence repeats as before where we lay side by side without touching. We didn't discuss our broken marriage on the five-hour hike to our empty beach, and we have barely spoken to one another at all these last three days. I am too ashamed to admit he is having an affair. Everyone in our small town will know—probably already knows—that I'm not worthy of love by my own husband. The truth is, I care more about what other people will think than about the actual end of the relationship.

Rain clouds swirl overhead as we set out on the difficult eight-mile hike back to the car the following morning. The trail weaves up the steep lava face, around unstable cliff edges, and over deep cracks. Camouflaged cairns, difficult to discern among the same colored background, lead finally to an easier to follow footpath in the semi-tropical forest.

"What do you think those owls meant?" I say, breaking the silence while we stop for a break. He looks back toward the ocean, black lava rock cut with gold fountain grass expand out below the steep trail.

"What did they mean?" he growls. "I don't know, they're just birds." I think back to how close they were to our faces, their wings getting caught in the palm fronds. They were speaking pretty clearly to me.

"You don't see owls every day," I reply. "Not that close. It meant something."

He looks at me, this time in agreement.

"They flew off in different directions," he quietly answers. "That's what I think it means." His ruddy complexion mirrors the brown landscape of the mountainside now below us.

I screw the cap back on my bottle as it begins to rain. He attempts to cover his pack with a plastic bag while cursing the weather. I hike on ahead. Red and pink ohia blossoms stand out brilliantly against the gray background of rain clouds and slick stone. Skinny trees dance as a light wind flutters their silvery, thumb-sized leaves. I don't know how much of this is magic and how much is real, how much is God and how much is my imagination. I've crossed over into the place the owl messengers flew off to.

It pours and pours. I have no hope that anything in my pack will stay dry. It doesn't matter. I hike ahead without looking to see if he is keeping up. Steam rises from smooth lava beds as the trail hits a clearing surrounded by giant tree ferns. The slippery rocks show no forgiveness, and I focus on taking one step at a time through fogged up glasses. Thunder crackles and lightning lights the way along the final stretch.

Opening the palms of my hands to the sky in gratitude to Lono, a Hawaiian god who communicates through the weather, I finally acknowledge the absolute power that rains from above. God brings the wonderful, warm rain. He sends the wind, the owls in the sky. He decides if we live or die, if volcanoes erupt, if a mountain falls. He can start and stop all these things. If this mysterious being has the power to move the clouds, push the wind and stir up the waves, why wouldn't He be able to intervene, somehow, in my tiny, scattered life? This blessed and beautiful life-giving rain was sent directly to me, to pour on my head, to keep me walking, up and away from the shadows lurking below.

WAR

THE WHITE STRIP OF paint is barely visible under a black sky as I slowly follow the roadside. He loves me, he loves me not, my feet slap out in rhythm. The dog's nails tick along the pavement and out beyond a scrubby field, the highway creeps along, red and white. Determined to put one foot in front of the other, my first baby steps toward freedom trail white hot behind.

Sand falls off my bare feet as I walk, the road flanked on both sides by fish farms. I don't look back toward him, at our lawn chairs and half-drunk beers sitting there by the ocean.

Give it a few minutes and he'll come barreling down the road to pick me up and further berate me for making him feel guilty. He can never make me happy, he says, and this is why he wants to leave. I've given so much for him, he says, and this is why he wants to leave. When did I go from being beloved to being pathetic?

I've given so much. I hadn't done anything wrong. I hadn't done anything right either.

The air, cool and constant, brings waves of salty breath. A pair of headlights flash ahead, illuminating my path and sending my shadow across the road. I don't wince or hesitate, only sip the air sharply, hoping these lights will meet my flesh. Hoping this long walk will end, now.

. . .

I couldn't see those footprints behind me glowing in the night, couldn't feel the very earth under foot blessing every movement forward. Without knowing it, the air and the earth and the stars all came together that night, pushing me along, guiding me forward. Preparing me for war.

PACKING LIGHT

(*optional)

- backpack
- camera
- water bottle
- courage*
- sleeping bag
- rain gear*
- good walking shoes
- warm weather clothes
- cold weather clothes
- outfit for going out
- good book
- pen and paper
- hat
- toiletries
- passport
- pedometer*

FEELINGS

I'M DRIVING MY CAR. In the backseat is a broody version of myself, full of anger and venom. Beside her is the over-reactive version, getting upset at every little personal offense. She won't shut up. Wounded me is there, too, weeping. It is crowded.

But the real me is driving. The confident, built from love, I am at my very core. I don't depend on those backseat hangers-on, I'm driving toward God. We pass a billboard, displaying an unkind letter from a loved one. I read it and keep driving. The backseat erupts in wounded cries, begging me to turn around so they can read it again. Not today.

As the sun goes down, I get a little break as my company in the backseat all fall asleep for the night. I keep driving down the empty highway in the desert, changing the CD every once in a while. A little Lyle Lovett, some Janis Joplin, a splash of the Bee

Gees. I roll the windows down, enjoying the solitude. When all is quiet, I can relax.

I drive all night and into the morning. With a yawn and a stretch, the others wake, blinking at me in the rearview mirror. Silent rage climbs into the front seat and starts trying to coax me into letting her drive. Not today. We pull into a diner and order coffees and pancakes. They all start talking at once, and I listen, not knowing what to do with them. Leave them here? They always find a way to catch up. I hold their hands, dry their tears, empathize, let myself feel. As they get warm-ups on coffee, they agree that dwelling on things doesn't get us there any faster. They ask me again where we're going.

A beautiful sun is rising in the east over peaks of golden mountains. God is over there, and I'm driving down a road that does not twist in that direction. Brooding me sees that I notice the mountains, and not for the first time. She tells me we need to get back on the road, that we're wasting time. Not today.

They climb back in and drive off, brooding me at the wheel. I swing my pack over my back and walk toward those golden mountains, leaving the road behind.

MYSELF

- Smart, kind, people like me.
- Hard-working, fair, empathetic, compassionate, romantic,
- Uncomplicated
- Cute, sweet, funny,
- Understanding, a good listener, in shape, healthy, organized, prepared,
- Obedient, patient, fun-loving, down to earth,
- Optimistic
- Hopeful, smiley
- Calculating, spontaneous, relaxed, knowledgeable, joyful, happy, serene,
- Artistic, creative, risk-taking
- Sensitive

SERENDIPITY

A COFFEE SHOP NEEDED an owner. This coffee shop was situated under a library in a small town in the mountains of Colorado. The kind of small town where twinkling lights dance over main streets and folks take their dogs to the post office. The kind of place visitors yearn to linger, wrapped in its sugar cookie quaintness. It is surrounded on all sides by tall, majestic, and utterly breathtaking mountains. Mountains that take on the color of moods, scenery that forces you to stop and look around. I was visiting a friend in this town who I'd met while walking the Camino de Santiago. I was on the move, on the run, not living anywhere, grounded to nothing after leaving my life in Hawai'i behind the year before. She mentioned this café, and I knew immediately it was waiting for me. After magically acquiring a rent-free lease for one year, I set about buying things like a cash register and furniture and heavy bottomed mugs. I brushed up on making espresso and mused over an impossible menu. It was almost as if I was gifted the cafe, was gifted a charming, real, yet hopelessly unreal, actual life. I dug right in and got to work.

Lovely people made their way to my basement brew house, bringing houseplants and pictures of their travels, outfitting me in snow boots and warm coats. In turn, I supplied them with breves (steamed half and half with espresso) for long ski days, lavender tea upon return, and fresh ground coffee to keep them coming back.

I rented a room, an A-frame joint with carpeted stairs, from my Camino friend. It was warm and cozy despite the persistent black mold in the shower and undercurrent of drama pervading the lives of the other humans inhabited there. The dog and I didn't mind. We woke up before the sun, crunching through frozen-over snow along a fast rushing stream before the start of very long work days. The only moments of peace and silence came before dawn, in that hour before the sun lit up the mountainside and sleepy customers made their way to my counter. I normally took a few minutes to brew a French press, sit at one of the tables made from antique doors, and write in a journal before beginning the day as barista/owner/ breathless over-worked business lady. Somedays, I headed outside as the sun rose for a deep breath or two. I had absolutely no idea what I was doing; the only option was to hold on tight.

We'd return home in the evenings, the dog and I, a bag of sweet potato chips in hand for dinner, walking alongside the stream again, this time the moon marking our steps. Stars in this kind of country are brighter and twinkle more than a thousand shining suns, which is of course, exactly what they are. Between working hours, my head would hit the pillow and that was all. It was all coffee, all the time.

Driving between mountains one evening after the nightly restocking shopping trip, an edgy purple sunset begged admiration. I pulled over and shuffled down a scraggly trail on the hillside. Below and in front, this pink and magenta mountain shone double in the reflection of Dillon Reservoir. The clouds gathered as if pulling over on their own journeys across the sky. I looked at that mountain and asked if she would please let me stay here, if she would please allow me to carve out a life in her stone.

• • •

This charmed life, this special gem of a circumstance, rolled out like a great rug of serendipity. The very stars had aligned and plopped this life in my lap. Yet, concurrently, and without know it, a trickle babbled alongside me, just flowing right along, exactly parallel to my currently rushing river. My river-path forked somewhere downstream, and before I knew it, I was floating down the trickle, watching the white water surge away, beyond the bank. I didn't even realize that I'd changed paths. I went right ahead steaming milk and paying bills with the little trickle moving me along, slowly but surely in another direction.

SPIRIT ANIMALS

Having never lived in a place that got much snow, the winter comes as quite a shock. I am terrified of driving and frustrated by walking. My dog limps every time we head outside. The act of scraping and clearing my car every morning, filling my boots with snow, and freezing my hands, becomes a steady burden.

One morning on the dark drive to work, a fox, cheerful and red, crosses my path. From there, a pattern quickly emerges. At the same intersection each morning, this fox darts out from the shadows right in front of my car. He doesn't look up or stop, just runs across the street. After seeing him numerous times, I research the fox, what he means historically to various cultures, his biological habits, trying to find some golden thread that connects us. A sense of panic consumes me every time this fox makes an appearance because, you see, the fox is a cross-cultural trickster in fables all around the world. It is clear he is a messenger, and surely, he is warning me. It can't be good.

. . .

There is half an inch of crunchy snow on the ground. The day's final colors backlight the branches of the leafless trees as I pick my way across the street and into the brewpub. I spot him right away despite his trendy glasses and tie over a patterned shirt. One hand on the table for balance, he stands to greet me with the same hesitant posture as always. He hugs me timidly, avoiding eye contact.

It has been a decade and then some since we last saw each other on the Chapman University campus in California. He is quite grown up now, no longer the skinny, goofy teenager I'd befriended my freshman year. We order beers and give updates on our lives. I relax into the conversation. It's not a date, just old friends having burgers.

Although we haven't spoken or written in all this time, neither of us are all that interested in rehashing old memories or talking about the past. This is a relief. Sometimes it feels like all I talk about is my recent split. Friends and family are constantly asking: How ARE you doing? What are your next steps? Have you heard from him?

Instead, we dive into the nuances of tasting beer, cooking techniques for the optimal french fry, and bad movies. The check comes, and we walk out into the snow together, coats buttoned tight. Bright red light from a sign down the block splashes the slush. He sees me looking and gestures toward it saying, "Have you ever been to the Thin Man?" I hadn't, but was always curious since I often frequented the coffee shop next door.

"Should we get a drink?" he asks.

"Why not?" I say and place a gloved hand through the crook of his elbow.

Inside is a collection of crucifixes and paintings of various bleeding Jesuses. The lighting is low, and there is a lot of red velvet and dark wood. We sit at a high-top table, and he orders some fancy cocktail I've never heard of; I get the mulled wine, on special. Talk quickly turns to the various ways the world should and could be saved. I slap the table more than once during a passionate soapbox. And I laugh, out loud, more than once at his well-timed jokes. The hot wine goes cold and forgotten.

We emerge, an hour later, back into the snow. "Let's do this again," I say. "Call me."

• • •

By the time the fox made his first dozen or so appearances, I am certain this man is the trickster. Not yet officially divorced from my ex in Hawai'i, I have no business getting into a new relationship. I have fallen absurdly, giddily in love with him, and the whole thing makes no sense and perfect sense at the same time. Our daring late night and early morning drives up and down the mountain to see each other become more and more frequent, distracting me from work. I worry that getting involved like this is self-sabotage, choosing a relationship over my newfound career goals. I start to notice that I'd gone down a fork in the river, bouncing down the trickle instead.

But resisting the rounds and rounds of Uno holed up in his sweltering top floor apartment is impossible. I make the two hour drive down on a Friday night for live music and dancing, only to drive back the next morning before sunrise. He calls in sick and drives up the mountain in a blizzard. We laugh a lot, and I try not to worry about what any of it means, even though that fox reminds me every single morning as it crosses the road.

Spring comes, and the snow, ever so slowly, begins to melt. He gets a job offer on the East Coast and picks up and moves. I put my head down and work endless hours, distraction-free. Mud season approaches quickly, and I close the shop to regroup and refresh, as many shop owners in mountain towns do at this time of year.

Spending a few days in Denver with my best friend, we go to a movie one night. I tell her about the fox and the trickster. We agree that maybe his far away move is for the best. She teases that it is crazy to think a fox might have warned me. On our way home that night, I look out the window while we wait at a stop light. With a loud laugh I grab her arm and point. There in the gutter, peering out at us, directly at us, is a little fox. We both scream with delight and confusion. The little trickster is back.

I take up my fox research once again as there must be something I missed. Foxes are solitary crea-tures. They do not roam in packs, preferring to hunt and skulk alone. They will cozy up to other foxes only when it is time to burrow in and have pups. I decide the message is that I am meant to roam alone.

I need to be alone.

Although it felt like it never would, the snow finally melts completely, even on the tops of the mountains. Spring flowers arrive, and I ride a yellow bicycle to and from the coffee shop, following the mountain spring once again. At the same time, the fast and furious love I'd fallen into turns into a long-distance relationship that keeps hanging on. We manage to see each other every month or so. Summer is busy at the coffee shop, and I draw up plans to expand, hire new people, and look ahead toward another winter.

• • •

None of which remotely works out. After a season of cold brew, long hikes, and whitewater adventures, it pinches to a close. Like an old TV set whose light fades to the center, this impossible light flickers out. My small staff all quit within days of each other, the long-distance thing became long and very distant, and I began to dread another year, another snowy winter, in the mountains. I packed up the heavy bottomed mugs, sell the tables and chairs, and headed out of town, by way of the clear, gurgling trickle.

SPIRALS

HERE I SIT AT a makeshift campsite in the mountains of Colorado on a weeknight. The sun just went down and even though it is summer, the temperature went with it. The dog and I are huddled by the fire. The truth is I'm homeless because the coffee shop is gone and I can't afford a place to live. For meals, I scrape together whatever I can find in my stash: tortillas with tahini or maybe oatmeal packets topped with peanut butter. I'm crying at this moment, sitting in the dark, because I'm right back where I started, on the move, on the run, grounded to nothing. Free from all direction, but trapped in a cycle.

Humility is a harsh teacher. I had been more concerned with what other people thought of my husband sleeping around than the actual end of my marriage. The thought of humiliation had me desperately clawing to keep that marriage upright. Over time, my outward facade became more important than my most valuable relationships. Even my goals centered on making my life seem the most adventurous and most ambitious. At the cost of the very bones of my soul. Humbled and humiliated at this, I finally gave in, and let what was to be, be. Even after learning all of this, I repeated history and let go of this surreptitious life here in the mountains, my coffee shop, for no reason at all. Except to be free.

There is still some color in the sky over the curve of the darkened mountain, a soft blue and orange mix. A few stars twinkle hello. The dog alerts to a flutter overhead, which I assume belongs to some bats passing through. He continues to stare into the waning light, and the beating wings return, this time lower.

This bird or bat swoops low over our campsite a few times before stopping to rest in a nearby tree where we can get a look at it. It's an owl, so close. It swoops low again, as if begging my attention. Another owl joins the first and they flutter together, circling each other, up toward the stars in the same direction. A warmness fills my chest. Again, they swoop low, one owl smaller than the other, alighting again in the tree, watching me for some time. It's not an endless loop I'm in; it's a spiral moving upward, toward something I cannot yet see, someplace these owls are headed, together.

TIME

Out past the pale gray sky, out past the tops of the buildings, past the forest and lakes. Way out to the mountains. One hundred years pass, then one thousand, looking down on a deepening valley, surrounded on all sides by snowless mountains. Ancient Bristlecone pines watch the passing of life. So many lives of green and of gold, of flesh and root, have died and sprung up again. And our lives, our footsteps that surround them now, are only one long breath, in and out, in the life of these trees.

As seeds, they chose this barren hillside. These pines are only found in the harshest plots of land. Each snowfall makes them stronger. A hard wind only begs them to stand taller, triumphant. Hundreds, perhaps thousands, of years these pines have thrived in this barren landscape.

I pick up a piece of bark the size of a large

grasshopper and pocket it, saying a little prayer for the pinecones full of seeds scattered among the boughs of the Bristlecone pines.

FATE

WOMEN ARE BORN WITH a lifetime of eggs in their ovaries. No more eggs are generated throughout their lives; they are only released. This child has been with me since the day I was born. She has always been part of me.

Now I have the wonderful, terrifying responsibility of forming an entire life. Of course, she is her own woman.

GRACE

Our footsteps mark a steady tune on the wet boardwalk in a little seaside town near Muxia, Spain. The tide is far out in the estuary, revealing large oyster shells in the sand among lots of plastic trash. The stones lining the water are coated in green slime. Behind us, an old castle, vacant now, draws tourists. Alice wanted to come to town with me to do the grocery shopping. I'm looking after a retreat house for pilgrims near Muxia, a popular destination for wayfarers looking to extend their journeys along the Camino de Santiago. The owner is gone for a month, entrusting me to look after the travelers, her house, and cats. My last great adventure for a long time, I suspect. Alice's cut-off green shorts reveal long and much-browned legs. Auburn hair curves around a youthful face. She is so light on the outside, so breezy and fun to talk with, so fresh on the inside. She's come all this way to northwest Spain to escape, to start again, to get sober on the Camino de Santiago pilgrimage. Cigarettes are the only thing she won't quit. I've only met her the day before after she wandered in, weary from walking.

Under the overcast sky, she tells me she was pregnant once. She didn't know until the bleeding started. Until it was too late to stop drugging and drinking, too late to decide to keep it or let it go. The weight she carries, the guilt, presses down on her every day. Pain radiates around her neck and shoulders as she tells me this. There is some higher power that gives and also takes away. We are powerless, we both agree.

As we walk on, I look around for my dog, who isn't with me since he's across the ocean. But it feels like someone else is walking with us. And I realize she is with us, enclosed in my womb, a constant companion. I imagine the pang Alice must have felt in her heart when her baby was lost. I pray I will be allowed to keep mine.

The next day, on a hike near the river, I find a purple quartz buried in the moss creeping over the path. I look up what purple quartz is used for, and it turns out some people use it to assist with sobriety.

I give it to Alice.

A month in the retreat passes, and Alice is long gone on her own journey. Morning sickness finally seizes me, and I am unable to walk back to Santiago on the Camino as planned, a three- or four-day journey heading inland, away from the ocean. Instead, I spend a couple days in a different pilgrim hostel in Muxia, right on the ocean, clinging to my bunk with terrible stomach cramps or laying limp on mossy stones near the shore, willing the waves to ease my nausea.

On the final morning before leaving Spain, a group of us travelers wait at a bus stop chatting about where we are from and why we are here. I explain to a young man my age that no, I hadn't walked any of the Camino this time around, that the morning sickness got the best of me in the end. A shadow cascades over his face, and he looks at his wife.

"You're pregnant?" he asks.

"Yes," I smile.

"My wife and I lost our baby a few months ago," he says softly. "He was three months old." He squeezes my hand.

I touch my womb without thinking, then look down at hers, at the pouch where she'd spent nine months nurturing a child who didn't live long in the world. I pray I will be allowed to keep mine.

MARRIAGE

WE GOT MARRIED ON Friday. I wore the purple dress with a clasp on the side that gathers the fabric over my barely visible bump. Mom sent us white roses, a tight bouquet wrapped in silk. We got to the downtown courthouse before 10 am. A young Asian clerk who refused to smile married us under a trellis decorated with fake pink roses. Our witness was a woman waiting for a court date. Within ten minutes of walking through the doors, we were signed, sealed, and delivered as Mr. and Mrs. People congratulated us on the street. A man with gold teeth agreed to snap our photo in front of the ornate black and metal courthouse doors.

We climbed into a cab afterward. With rushed voices, we told the driver to take us to the waterfront where there is a row of shops and restaurants. The Mt. Vernon section of Baltimore is full of beautiful old churches and stone facades to admire as we pass through downtown. Most storefronts are unoccupied or clumsily lit with signs for liquor or sub sandwiches.

We exchanged polite hellos with the driver. "Are you married?" he wanted to know.

We exchanged glances then, silently deciding whether or not to share that we'd gotten married that very day, in the courthouse up the road.

"Yes, we're married," my new husband replied.

"That's very good!" the driver said. "Many couples who get in my cab are not married. I don't like that."

He gave a long speech about how to get along in marriage. His crucial point was to take a drink of cold water when you get upset. He said if you bend too much, you will eventually break. We just listened.

LETTING GO

- The journal I'd kept on the Camino, stuffed
  with pressed flowers and herbs
- My sturdiest pair of heels
- A pink A-line dress that fit just right
- Every piece of jewelry I'd ever owned
- An immersion blender
- My Bible
- Every journal entry written about running a
  coffee shop

After leaving Colorado, I mailed many of my journals, books, and other personal things in big boxes to a PO Box in Baltimore. They never arrived. The tracking number said they'd made their way to some kind of lost mail depot in Georgia. Perhaps the boxes fell apart or I'd written the wrong address.

Either way, after submitting a long, handwritten list of all the items in the boxes, they were still never recovered.

PIEDAD

I am not Catholic. On the day before leaving Hawai'i and toward the Camino in Spain, I came upon a statue of Our Lady of Guadalupe in a garden. The plaque promised that those who prayed to her would gain protection. I prayed.

On my first day in Spain, I stumbled upon a church of her namesake. Again, I prayed to her for protection.

. . .

After completing the Camino, I made my way to Denver. The journey to find a new home began to edge into the territory of simply being lost, I was scared and took long walks through parks and neighborhoods to clear my mind. I passed a church. A sharp-eyed hawk lived in the steeple. I decided to stop for Mass. It was the feast day of Our Lady of

Guadalupe. The parishioners passed out little cards with her image and a short prayer on the back. I keep this card in a special place with other letters and images I cherish.

After finding out about my pregnancy, I bought a candle with her image and prayed for the protection of unborn children, of my unborn child. She especially favors unborn children, according to the printed label on the candle.

We searched for a home in Baltimore for many months. Some were too big or too small, some had too many stairs or too many bidders. When I was seven months pregnant, we walked down the street to an open house on a cold February evening. This house was spacious, but not too large. It had lovely, large windows and high ceilings. We loved it, but it was not quite what we had in mind. As we shook hands with the realtor upon leaving, I noticed a stack of cards laying on the staged coffee table. They were business cards for a local psychic emblazoned with the image of Our Lady of Guadalupe. Mary herself had left me a message.

We live here now, all three of us, tucked neatly under Mary's cloak, the card and the candle taking up residence on my nightstand.

AWE

ON THE FIRST SUNRISE of my daughter's life, I opened the front door to a sky dotted with rain clouds.

"It's a new day for you," I whispered.

Her open eyes peered out from a swaddle of gauze, her little hands tightly closed. Across the street, the gray, white, and light blue sky began to change to vibrant colors from the rising sun, over the pitch of the nearby Presbyterian church. She gazed at the sky in the same way I gazed at her face, with wonder and amazement at these things we have never seen before.

THE SONG OF MY HEART

SHE IS GROWING SO fast that we will probably forget the way her shiny glass eyes peer out from a squishy face. We will forget how cute and soft her little noises are, her wide yawn, her impossibly tiny fingernails. She will grow and grow, and very quickly her hair will turn from down to soft curls to textured locks. Her mouth will go from soft pink to full of teeth to crooked smile. I will forget what it felt like to carry her in my belly, the pain of birth, the anticipation of seeing her face for the first time.

This time will pass, like all things do, beautiful and tragic. We will never again have a tiny infant Ella to croon over while she sleeps, weeks of rain keeping us indoors, hours and hours just to hold her and rock her and admire her ears and eyebrows and toes. So that leaves nothing else to do but just savor this day, this entry into Motherhood. To take some time to be thankful for answered prayers that were so precious, they were never spoken aloud.

I never thought that it would feel this way. Like standing on a mountain top, having walked for weeks and weeks. Like having customers fill a coffee shop. Like locking the door to my Hawaiian home for the last time and not looking back. That glorious sense of free fall when you take a chance on something your heart pulls you toward. That realization that this is the song of your heart. That moment of knowing I was made for this.

ANGELS

ELLA IS NAMED AFTER an angel. I knew she was a girl after hearing her heartbeat for the first time. Her grandmother died three years before she was born, and it felt right and perfect to name her after the woman who I knew already to be hanging around as her guardian angel.

In a Spanish bookstore during my final adventure before having her, I flipped through a guidebook on angels and saints. There was an entry on seraphim and cherubim, Biblical angels. The seraphim's wings burn with an inextinguishable light for charity, enlightening others in the process.

While eating lunch with a dear friend and little Ella Seraphim, a man passing by stops in his tracks to insist, "You know that baby is an angel? A real angel." He is a grandpa type, with very bright eyes. He says, "God bless," when he leaves us.

He is an angel, too, of course.

STAYING PUT

THE WOMAN AT THE social security office looks me right in the eyes, pained.

"I'm sorry," she offers in genuine sympathy as she approves the paperwork to change my last name back to my maiden name.

The divorce was light years behind me by then, and I was barreling hard and fast into a new life. I'd shown the world that nothing could stop me, proven that I was whole. I'd ripped my life into a million pieces and put them all back together again.

"You've proven your point," my sister breathes into the phone, as older siblings do. She's right, as older siblings are. But is it enough?

I pray for the bravery and strength it takes to eat dinner every night at the same time and be glad in it.

It's time to slow down and take it all in.

FREEDOM WARRIOR

It's time to stop running and soak in the bath.
Time to learn to enjoy the everyday and not just
the big, splashy entrances and exits.

GRATITUDE

- a fun kid to play with
- food in the cupboard
- dust on my shoes
- a quiet moment with coffee
- green tea
- the space between there and here

It is still 80 degrees at 9 pm. I walk the dog to the park. A deep pink sunset grazes the tall buildings of downtown Baltimore. Underneath the cherry and oak trees, fireflies begin to swirl. Little sparkles that you catch out of the corner of your eye.

A little girl pushes her scooter past us on the concrete trails, remarking that her mom won't let her have a dog. An ice cream truck sings. Other kids play ball shirtless in the alley.

As it gets darker, the soccer field becomes carpeted by tiny firefly lights.

FACING FEARS

I WAS INFORMED YESTERDAY that my child's father will be deployed to the Middle East for almost a year. He will miss a year of her life. He will miss her first birthday, her first steps, her first words.

My instinct is to run, untethered. Get me away from here. Take me to a sheltered place away from this crumble-brick city with overflowing buses. Hide me, hide us, away from the fear that I, alone, will not be enough for this child. I cannot be enough for her. I cannot sit here and do this, firmly planted in this life.

RUNNING

I'M STILL HERE. SITTING here. In the same old bed about to put on the same old shoes. There is a TV program on about nothing in particular. I wish beyond wishes to get out of this place. I tidy up the bed, put water on to boil, and tie my shoes. It's a sunny day outside, dreadfully hot; it might as well be the desert. But it's not. It's the middle of the city: brick, concrete, weeds growing in cracks. I wish beyond wishes to be doing something else. I snap up my pocketbook, pour boiling water over a tea bag in a travel mug, and head out the door. Today, I will start a new life, I say. Run away. So I get some cardboard boxes after quitting my job and start packing up my life. Into storage it goes. I pay the landlord last month's rent. I sell the couch and bed and buy a yellow bicycle. The goldfish gets dropped off at my sister's.

The bike takes me out of the city, away, away, until the drab little room is a speck behind me. I pedal and pedal, passing many, many sights. A canyon, a forest, a pumpkin farm. I see an old Honda hatchback for sale by the side of the road and buy it with what's left in my bank account. Now I can really zoom past fields and meadows, through cities and farms. Faster and faster, away, away.

I stop for a snack of cheese and crackers and spot a brilliantly colored hot air balloon for sale. After much discussion, a woman trades it for the bike and the car.

I fire up the balloon and into the sky it lifts until the car is gone and the land is something entirely new. I sail over rivers and lakes and the sea. I spy terrifying waves and storm clouds. Mountains fit into the palm of my hand.

Just then, a rocket ship lifts off from its pad, and I abandon the balloon, grab hold of the rocket, and hold on tight. Up, up, faster, faster, away, away. In a flash, the whole world is in the dust I leave behind. I marvel at the small blue marble world as the rocket sails around it, landing on a nearby satellite. The stars are so bright, the air is so cold.

A comet comes splicing toward me, and I grab

its vibrant tail as it soars past the world and out into the galaxy. I hop from comet to comet this way, dancing among the stars. I see constellations no one has ever seen before. Around and around, up, up, faster, faster, away, away. Until the solar system itself is just a speck of dust.

I finally find a place to rest on a tired old moon that another planet isn't using anymore. That's when I notice the thread behind me, attached to me. The golden ribbon that has followed me all this time.

I pull on the ribbon. And pull and pull and pull, until the whole universe moves toward me and my old solar system comes into view. My world still spins steadily on its axis. I pass the satellite I stopped at before, pulling the thread, pulling, pulling, pulling until I am gliding among the clouds once again. I pass my hot air balloon, left drifting somewhere over China. I pull and I pull on the ribbon and now my feet have touched the ground. Still I keep pulling this thing, knowing where it will lead, knowing that I must keep pulling.

I pull myself along, past the fields and meadows, and back into the city. I walk up the three stories to my old room and old bed, still waiting for me.

I crawl under my glorious covers and fall fast asleep, right where I belong.

TRANSFORMATION

THE MESSAGE AT ELLA'S baptism:

Jesus said, "Take up your cross and follow me. For whoever wants to save his life will lose it, but whoever loses his life for me will save it."

Matthew 16:24–25.

She is babbling during the sermon, and it feels like Jesus is speaking directly to me. Becoming a mother, my life for hers, means I am no longer the same woman. My holy purpose is to raise this girl the best I can. I have resisted this tethering, wanting to stay the same person, wanting to remain separate from her. I have no choice; I am forever changed. I choose to pick up the cross and follow. I choose her.

• • •

The old me has perished. Everything I knew has blown away or dissolved. Now, I stand in a well-lit room, stark white, a blank canvas, with no one around and nowhere to go. There is a box of paint, some brushes. It is time to start again.

HERE AND NOW

THIS GIRL, ASLEEP IN my arms, is so beautiful. Her dark waves, imperfect brows, round nose, golden skin. She is me but not me. She is God but not God.

Yesterday was our last night together as a family. It went as it usually does. I fell asleep soothing the baby, forgetting to brush my teeth. He's gone now. As soon as he pulled out of the driveway, we went for a walk in the sunshine. The city streets were quiet and nice. When we came home, I just sat, sort of stunned. Trying to think of little things I could do around the house, but mostly staring out the upper window into the bright blue afternoon.

I feel sad. I no longer have anything to hold onto but a clean house.

FAILURE

DUSK HAD PASSED, AND night is descending all around us. The highway back to Portland twists and turns its way through farmlands, prime deer-in-headlights territory. Cars used to this kind of driving pass me, over the double yellow, without hesitation. The baby screams in the backseat, my fingers turning white from squeezing the steering wheel.

I had just left a book club dinner meeting in which a posh and retired women's group had gouged my book without saying a word. We'd dined al fresco: chicken, salad, and cake. The baby nursed while I gave a short photo slideshow and tried to smile with every eye in the room glaring at me. Who knows what they were actually thinking. But they barely spoke a word to me, barely tried at a question. Their white pleated pants and chunky turquoise jewelry complemented the custom upholstered couches, the tailored curtains. My ex-mother-in-law had convinced me to come and visit. She wanted to see the baby, and I had selfishly agreed, given I could share my newly published book with her book club friends. I was desperate to be something other than a mother. She had gushed over the book, so however awkward, I thought there was a good chance the book club would like it, too. It was another way to prove my point that I had moved on, successfully, into a new life.

I was sorely wrong. We are on the freeway now, and the baby has finally fallen asleep. She has endured a long day of driving to be here. For nothing. My sense of panic increases as every shadow along the roadway looks like a deer about to careen into the truck, which sets into motion that terrible, ugly inner voice. "Who are you to write a book? Did you really think they would like it? And what kind of mother are you anyway, exposing her to that situation with your ex-family? What's more important, a book or a baby?" Critical me sits in the passenger seat, taunting me all the way. They always return.

I am a jerk. And of course it is getting late, after 9 pm, way past the baby's bedtime. I am driving back to my brother-in-law's place, tucked into a wooded mountain in Portland. The turns become tighter as we ascend the mountain. I slam on the breaks as a dark figure darts out in front of me. It stops in the ditch to turn and show its face.

A fox. This time, I take the message differently. I have burrowed in, like the solitary fox is known to do, and had a pup. He was not a trickster, but rather, an oracle.

MERCY, AGAIN

WE CAUGHT A MOUSE this morning. His legs were twisted up in a glue trap, struggling to get free. I commanded the dog to take him outside. He did, leaving it at the bottom of the stairs. I hoped the dog had killed it, or that it would die soon.

Many hours later, I go out the backdoor to get into the car, baby seat in both arms. The mouse is still there, on the trap, still struggling to get free. My thoughts whirl. I don't want him to endure more suffering. I think about running inside to grab a bowl of water to drown him. No, too cruel. I grab the trap; he is so delicate and cute. I can see his chest and stomach exploding with breath and heartbeat. I put him in the small black compost tin and close the lid. Surely the heat will kill him eventually, he will definitely suffocate. I finish putting the baby in the car and roll down the windows. Just before taking off, I hop back out, grab the mouse, and throw him in the trash can. This will kill him faster since the can has been in the hot sun all morning.

His tortured little legs haunt my thoughts as I drive. Only later did it occur to me that I could have pried him loose to release him. He didn't have to die at all.

. . .

When I was nine or ten years old, my parents let me get two pet mice. They lived in a little glass aquarium with a wheel to run on and bark dust to nestle into. Being nine or ten, I was really bad about remembering to feed them. One day, I went to check on them, and they were gone. I opened the metal grate to their cage and began searching under their wheel and toys. I found them, half-decomposed, buried in the bark dust.

. . .

Several hours later, when we return home, I pray the mouse is dead. I lift the lid and spot him, eyes wide open, lifeless. I hope he died peacefully, but I know that he didn't. I have added to the suffering of the

world and am now convinced my karmic wheel just
spun in the wrong direction.

ASKING FOR HELP

Yesterday was my birthday. That afternoon, I loaded up the stroller with sodas, the diaper bag, cleats, and a glove to play softball in the park with church friends. I brought the baby and dog along. I don't really know the church people all that well, and there's no way for them to know that I'm on my own right now with the baby and a dog and a house and care taking and dishes.

There was one lady willing to watch Ella for a bit, but she wasn't thrilled about it. In the two innings I got to play, I dropped a grounder, chickened out on catching a fly ball, and struck out. And the dog ran out onto the field. The baby lay happily in the grass, looking up at the shadows of leaves dancing in the trees. Afterward, I begged some folks to take the sodas so I wouldn't have to carry them back. My bags were heavy, but losing the sodas didn't lighten the load. I cried the whole walk back home. Another friend came over to eat pizza and watch Miss America in the evening. She was worried about me and asked how she could help. I didn't know how to answer except that I needed to go to bed early.

· · ·

The toothpaste tube rests on the edge of the sink bowl, dented and smashed from tip to end. I pick it up, unscrew the cap, and squeeze gently with my entire palm. Only when it becomes difficult to squeeze, after palming it for weeks, will I roll it up neatly, pressing the remaining paste toward the exit.

· · ·

The woman at Target gave me a discount when my debit card wouldn't go through. It's true I'm out of money, but I didn't deserve that kindness. She's the one working her ass off at Target. I thanked her and only hope to pay it forward.

SIMPLICITY

WE WALKED TO TWO RIVERS PARK again this morning. Stopped for a beautiful, quiet moment sitting on the bench in front of a whitewashed and peeling door that opens to someone's private courtyard. I was transported to another country, another place, far away. A place where the shade cools and comforts me, where sweet smelling flowers bloom and lemons drip from trees. A place between the real and the imagined. Ella slept peacefully in her carrier. A woman in a housedress and ankle high nylons came out to feed the pigeons pieces of bread. She did not stop to watch them enjoy it, just turned and walked back into her house.

I enter liminal space by:

- hearing drumming on an abandoned beach
- leaving coffee in fairy-sized mug, gone by the next morning
- swimming in golden pools of brackish water
- washing my hair in a waterfall
- walking among ancient Bristlecone pines
- waking during the witching hour at the same moment as the baby
- witnessing the rise of a full, purple moon
- picking pottery off of the ground, crafted thousands of years ago

Perhaps, being a baby is also existing in a thin place, in the betwixt, all the time. One day, I'll look back on my luminous past and smile. And shine, just shine. One day.

SURVIVAL

Things I do to pass time:

- craft
- paint/write quotes and affirmations
- listen to affirmations
- hang artwork
- organize
- pot plants
- watch rom-coms
- move furniture around
- read
- wait for fairies
- pray with a tiny shell between my palms

Methods I use for self-care:

- sleep with my phone off or away from the bedside
- take a few moments a day to sit in my bed with my cup of tea
- meditate
- pray
- consume less sugar, less caffeine, less meat
- drink more water
- don't let money control me (money comes and money goes)
- care for my skin
- accept the situation

GETTING UP

I'M SITTING CROSS-LEGGED ON the couch with a half cup of tea between my hands. It's one of those mugs that's more like a bowl, white with a floral print. Orange spice tea with honey lingering at the bottom steams upward. The pale pink orange drink is almost gone. I close my eyes and imagine the cup full again, imagine manifesting this with my mind.

After a few moments, I open my eyes, walk to the tea kettle, and fill my own cup. Water is easy to come by.

UNLOADING

I'M ON A TRAIL with a giant pack weighing heavily on my tired shoulders. It slides off with a slump as I stop to unload extra clothes and the DSLR camera that captured each scenic point beautifully, but also each misstep and impasse in too crisp of a focus. These items can wait for new owners now, among the brambles and thick mint growing along the path. With my lightened load, I set off again, my neck still aching from the heavy load.

PEACE

Peace Prayer of Saint Francis

Lord, make me an instrument of your peace:
where there is hatred, let me sow love;
where there is injury, pardon;
where there is doubt, faith;
where there is despair, hope;
where there is darkness, light;
where there is sadness, joy.

O divine Master, grant that I may not so much seek
to be consoled as to console,
to be understood as to understand,
to be loved as to love.
For it is in giving that we receive,
it is in pardoning that we are pardoned,
and it is in dying that we are born to eternal life.
Amen.

Perfection is a cup of coffee and a sleeping babe. The coffee is actually still hot. I love being the only one awake in the house. Even the dog is snoring. Surely we must let the magic happen on its own or we don't really believe. God, I accept this path as Your will for me. It is my duty and honor to raise my daughter, to be the best mother I can. I won't worry about spoiling her or what other people think; I'll just let Your love shine through me. Tear down my resistance.

• • •

She just smiled in her sleep—is she listening to my thoughts?

IMPOSSIBILITIES

I'VE BEEN TOLD TO set the stage for napping, to embark on a strict routine that signals to the child that now is the time to sleep. Although I know she is exhausted, this child will not sleep. For weeks, I've diligently kept to the routine. First feed, then rock, then turn on the same gentle music each day at exactly the same time. She will not sleep.

• • •

She lies next to me on the bed and wiggles or fusses until I finally pick her up again. Her eyes finally grow heavy and then gently, gently, I set her down to sleep, holding my breath and tiptoeing down the stairs to get more coffee in the 30-second window I have, when her brain hasn't yet registered that I'm not there. I slide back to my post on the bed, careful not to disturb her slumber. I let out a sigh of relief for this precious, short break from being a mom. I haven't eaten yet and begin peeling an orange slowly. Her eyes flutter open, and she begins to whimper. The orange hits the opposite wall with enough force to split the fruit open. Juice drips down toward the carpet, and a sound leaves my mouth that can only be described as anguish.

LONELINESS

THERE WERE DAYS THIS winter, like this one, when the only exposure I had to the outside world was a quick run across the street to let the dog roam around the church yard. Ella is bundled in her fleece suit and hat, cozy in the front-loading carrier, my heavy winter coat zipped over her. The wind bites us as I try to throw sticks for the dog.

I'll admit I am a total slave to her naps. I crave the time to myself, time without anyone touching me or looking at me. I'm like a dog who hasn't eaten all day. I'm so lonely but never alone.

I need to be away from this. I need to escape.

I need to accept this. I need to accept her.

I need to be courageous. I am brave right now by just breathing in and out. By putting food in my mouth and sweeping the floors and steadily going through the motions of mothering and housekeeping.

Hard is not impossible.

PARADOX

I AM LONELY BUT never alone. I am brewing lavender and mint tea. Life is simple, yet difficult. Nothing's coming out right. Be positive. Be real, honest. I have failed at everything, yet I am somehow a success. I desperately need a break from the baby, but can't bear to leave her. I doubt myself each step of the way, but my stride says otherwise. Push–pull. Yin–yang. Opposites can co-exist. I want my freedom, but I don't want to walk through life alone.

MAGIC

On Christmas Eve she refuses to go to sleep, like any child on such a night, so we walk the one block to our church on Clinton Street. It is a warm and still night; many row houses we pass lit up with lights. She keeps looking at the sky, but there are no stars to show her.

After we arrive, I eat a cookie with a cup of coffee in the church basement and say hello to the handful of parishioners who also made their way here. In the sanctuary, we sit in the back and wait for the service to start. Ella is dazzled by the lights and the luminous stained glass. She leans back to nurse, and I look up at an image of Mary holding her baby much like I am doing now. We make it for about half of the service before she screams for her bed. Walking back home on this silent night, I whisper to her the story of Christmas.

After she is safely tucked in, I have a little eggnog and watch the end of A Christmas Story. The house is more than quiet. I think about Santa Claus and what I should tell Ella when she is older. Should I encourage a belief in Santa? This year at least, she is too young to remember either way. The practical side of me remembers the crush of finding out it was my parents leaving the gifts all along. The magical side wonders if he could be real after all. In the kitchen, there is a tiny plastic tea cup and saucer on the windowsill. I sometimes remember to leave a little coffee for the kitchen fairies. Washing it out, I fill the cup with a eggnog and find a cookie to nestle in the saucer. It all gets tucked under the tree, just in case.

Christmas morning is bright, and we are up very early. A small tree in a yellow flower pot sits on the end table next to the couch. It is strung with white lights and a few sparkly ornaments. Ella is just beginning to crawl and can scoot backward wherever she wants to go. I put the fairy cup of eggnog in the sink to wash later and find her under the tree among the presents friends and family have sent from all over the country. Snapping a few pictures of this sweet moment, we wait for her dad to come online to video chat.

He watches her open all her gifts. The ones with tissue paper are her favorite. No extra gifts from Santa appeared since the night before. I pull up the photo of her under the tree to send to him and notice several little white dots surrounding her in the picture. It looks like little magic fairy lights dancing around her head.

We eat breakfast, put on the matching outfits my mother sewed for us, and drive to Pennsylvania. Friends invited us to their family Christmas out near Lancaster. Theirs is an old brick home with lots of children and food and dogs. We can all fit at the large dining table, set beautifully with candles and flowers. We eat prime rib and Jell-O salad and buttery mashed potatoes.

Ella loves the other children and plays right through her nap. After some of the excitement dies down and the big kids are off watching a movie, the lady of the house announces she has gifts for Ella. A beautiful new outfit. A set of large Legos. A stuffed bear with rings and flags to pull and squeeze. These gifts are the nicest she got today. There is one for me, but I hide it behind my back, embarrassed, and plan to open it later. I didn't bring any gifts to reciprocate. I am astonished at their kindness. The feeling stings the back of my throat. I hold the tears in until the lonely drive back, Ella crying all the way home, too.

After coaxing her to sleep at home, I go back to the car to unload the diaper bag, coats, and gifts. Inside the little box for me is a cross necklace. It is the exact same style as the one I wore on my Camino de Santiago pilgrimage two years before, the year God found me. Sitting by my Christmas tree with the last of the eggnog, I toast to Santa. He had, in fact, come for us.

LIGHT

I HOLD A TINY flame close to my heart, even though this persistent fire will not be blown out. A gust of wind, a gale force storm, only bends the flame from side to side, holding fast to its wick. Bare feet find their way forward in the darkness, winds whipping through thin clothes as I carry this flame.

During the storm, a spark flies off into the blackness, igniting, one by one, a dozen other flames. I don't see these flames up close, can only see, from a distance, how the fire spreads, glowing brightly on the horizon. I trudge on, cupping my treasured flame with hands brittle from the cold. Lugging a heart so heavy, so disgraced.

I find some newspaper, tucking it under dry branches. The paper burns brightly for a few moments from my flame, but fails to ignite the wood. This happens again and again, day after day.

FREEDOM WARRIOR

Some days I don't even try. The fuel is there. The fire is there. Yet, nothing.

Still, the flame persists, tiny as it is.

RESOLUTIONS

As I WRITE THIS, my perfect, two-toothed little girl is sleeping beside me. Bright mid-morning sunshine filters through the curtains, and the coffee has not yet gone cold. Watching her sleep while I furiously write in a journal has been the greatest hit of this year, and I'll never tire of these sweet, fleeting moments.

We settle into nap time by listening to a collection of her dad's old CDs, from a time when CDs were their own currency. Sometimes, I tiptoe downstairs after she closes her eyes for another cup of coffee, but usually I sit next to her, propped up with pillows, savoring that soft in and out of her breath.

• • •

There have been so many peaceful, serene moments this year. The kind that are easily forgotten. Sunrise on an abandoned beach in Virginia, snow coating the sand. Fall colors from the blustery top of Prospect Mountain. Beignets and cups of coffee from white saucers in New Orleans while watching Spanish moss drip its own sweat. The entire month of rain after Ella was born in which we sat on the couch and stared at her lovely face for hours and hours and hours. Sitting on a bench in the tiny neighborhood park I discovered nestled in an alleyway, joined only by an older man who gave a treat to my dog with joyful gusto. The crab feast we hosted for family and friends featuring a giant steaming box of Old Bay encrusted creatures.

Watching the effect a baby has on humanity is equal parts surprising and gut-wrenching. A woman at the post office gave me ice cream money for Ella when she was two months old. A rough-looking man stopped to stroke her face and hair with such tenderness that tears flooded my eyes. A group of moody teenage boys sitting next to us in church couldn't help but put down their phones and take turns making her smile.

· · ·

Ella fell asleep in my arms around 8 pm on New Year's Eve after I turned on It's a Wonderful Life.

She knew it was a holiday and tried to stay awake. I take her to bed, light a candle, and pour two glasses of champagne, one for me and one for my love half way across the universe. If I were away from this baby for as long as he has been, I know I'd die of heartache. I pray that his heart aches a little less today. Finishing most of our homemade pizza, I climb up the stairs to bed around 10 pm.

The booms of midnight fireworks wake both me and Ella. She lifts her little head and gives a giant smile. I scoop her up in my arms and take my midnight kiss. I nurse her back to sleep to the reflection of fireworks sparkling in the neighbor's windows. Now that, my friends, was a good year.

EXPECTATIONS

I HAD A REALLY tough week at work. My co-workers were annoying, my boss gave me more work than I could physically complete, and the kid was sick. All week I dreamed of heading to my favorite pub on Friday for a juicy BBQ burger with onions and cheddar cheese paired with a beer and some house-made chips. It was the only thing getting me through the week.

Friday finally arrives, and I manage to duck out of work a little early to meet a friend at the pub. I order my juicy BBQ burger with onions and cheddar cheese and lean into the high-back chair sipping a well-earned beer. The server comes back to the table bearing heavy platters. He sets a large, beautifully pink prime rib steak in front of me.

I push my chair back from the table a little, hands up, and declare that I'd ordered a juicy BBQ burger with onions and cheddar cheese. My friend has already taken a bite of hers. The server explains that they've run out of burgers but the chef sent out this much better steak instead, no charge.

I look at the large, beautifully pink prime rib steak. It looks tasty, but I've been waiting on that burger, wanting my juicy BBQ burger with onions and cheddar cheese, all week. Disappointment sags my shoulders. The waiter explains again that there are no more burgers. Time slowly ticks by.

I'm unsure what to do now. Walk out of the restaurant? Convince my friend to share hers? Or perhaps, maybe, possibly, accept that the burger is not going to happen tonight and enjoy this far superior steak.

NAPPING

May 1, 2016

I thought Ella would be born today. Now she's almost a week old. We were up all night; she wouldn't fall asleep. Right now, her little head fits in my hand, she'll never be this small again. Motherhood is a secret song. A prayer I thought I shouldn't even pray.

September 15, 2016

Today I went for a walk because I didn't know what else to do for Ella. I was waiting for her to nurse, but she kept getting fussier and fussier; it is so hard to get her to nap. Instead of our usual route to the park, I decide to walk some quiet side streets. It is hard to escape the city noises, which make me feel even more overwhelmed. I cried all day.

September 21, 2016

Been in crisis mode a lot lately. Everything feels like an emergency. Everything feels like it's too much. Got up early because I couldn't sleep anymore. Ella is still upstairs. We are supposed to go to an outdoor concert tonight and I'm dreading staying out late. I protect my sleep like a lioness. And then I can't sleep.

November 2, 2016

"Go to sleep, go to sleep," I plead. Inside, I want to scream for my lack of rest. I've been alone with the baby for a week. Inwardly, I'm in a rage, although I know this is completely irrational. My insides don't match my outsides, never have.

December 17, 2016

7 pm	fell asleep (crying)
8 pm	woke up
9 pm	back to sleep (screaming)
9:30 pm	woke, fed
11:30 pm	woke, screaming, fed
1 am	woke, screaming, gave meds
2 am	woke
2:30 am	woke, fed

4 am woke, off and on until 6 am
6 am fed
6:45 am woke for the day

December 21, 2016

Shortest day of the year. Absolutely no sleep. Ella is up every 15–30 minutes until 2:30 am when she is wide awake until 5 am, after which she will only sleep upright in my arms.

December 24, 2016

Been thinking about Mary. It is a miracle she wasn't killed. It really is a miracle that Jesus was born. We don't need to be in Pennsylvania until 2 pm tomorrow, which is, of course, Ella's nap time. Only a little nervous about the drive. But I can do anything for 45 minutes. Please God don't let there be traffic.

December 25, 2016

Ella is eight months old today. We saw three hawks on the way to Pennsylvania. On lucky days, I wake before Ella and can write by the light of the sunrise. It is so dark in the morning.

December 31, 2016

This year hasn't been all bad. There were a lot of firsts: Mother's Day, Halloween, Thanksgiving, Christmas. First child, first home together. First baptism, first dip in the Atlantic, first trip to New Orleans. Thank you, God, for another beautiful year.

January 1, 2017

We have mice in the house. I've found droppings in the kitchen, behind the changing table, and even on the couch. Last night, I had a dream that the dog and I were standing in the kitchen and he couldn't even catch the mice that were standing in the middle of the floor. If mice come into your life, it means you are missing details right in front of you, I looked it up on a spirit animals website. Today, I called the exterminator. He made the mistake of asking if there were mice upstairs, which I hadn't yet considered. And now I lie in bed, awake, imagining mice nesting in my bed, in my couch, swarming over the dishes and baby's toys, contaminating everything.

January 20, 2017

I'm not going to withhold my dreams because of obligation. I'm going to live richly and fully. God has given me everything I need to do so in this very moment. I only need to choose it.

Right now, I have a cup of tea. My best friend is on her way for a visit. I can call or text A any time. I am watching my baby turn into a kid. It is exhausting, but one day I will wish to do it all again. I miss my freedom. Quite a lot. Quite, quite, quite. But this is a new kind of freedom, isn't it? What if I just let go? Lift my head and laugh? What if we just play together and cuddle and cry together?

Janduarry 22, 2017

I don't love breastfeeding in public. The thought of someone catching a glimpse of my enlarged and brown nipple is really uncomfortable. But I do it as my daily protest. Yesterday, we marched down Independence Avenue in Washington, D.C. at the Women's March. We didn't need to raise our fists to demand respect. We simply showed up, raised our hands and voices to say enough. We are here. You will see us.

January 24, 2017

Magic moments. Was able to sneak downstairs to make coffee, and now I'm writing in the dim light of dawn. Placed a water glass on the window sill so that just enough reflected prisms can pass by the curtain. Ella is asleep by my side.

February 26, 2017

It's a sunny February day. I've made and eaten breakfast, swept the floors, and written in this journal. Ella sleeps in late these days. What I really want to say is this: I am ecstatic to be Ella's mom, and I have been treating this role as less than that. Have been mourning the loss of my independence, autonomy, and freedom. Let it go, let it die. I will reemerge better for this.

March 18, 2017

I'm up before Ella, having coffee and sitting by the fire. However brief this lasts, I'm happy. She was up every hour last night. We are staying in a cabin in West Virginia at a writer's retreat. There is a kitchen table and a coffee pot, a fireplace and wood paneling, what else can I really ask for? It feels like I've found the house by the creek that I've always wanted, or it found me, or God led me to it. Or all of these things at once.

March 23, 2017

I've got the porch light and back deck light on. The house alarm is set. I have a roommate in the finished basement. The dog barks not only when someone knocks but if someone walking by is too close to the front stoop. Yet still I leap out of bed at any unusual sound, making sure the bedroom door is locked and my phone is within arm's reach.

April 1, 2017

My baby will be one this month. Right now I am sitting at the dining table while she studies her books very intently, picking them up one by one, turning each page, stopping to wonder. She looks up at me and smiles. The eggs are getting cold, but the coffee is hot, and I'm not going to disturb her. The morning light through the window catches her face and hair just so.

April 16, 2017

Being alone with this baby is like heaven and hell. My moods change rapidly each day, waking to a serene, happy baby who then screams before each nap, then joyfully dances to our favorite music. I furiously clean up after she dumps the dog's water (again). It's exhausting, this loneliness. I'm furious for being impatient. I'm furious for feeling sorry for myself.

May 2, 2017

I drank two cocktails last night and forgot to do the laundry. Don't know why I did that except I just wanted to feel like I could. Ate all the crackers and peanut butter.

June 5, 2017

I'm afraid I am a cold, weak mother. I'm afraid my instincts aren't good. I've been sleeping really poorly lately, jumping out of sleep because I'm afraid she is falling off the bed. Some of that old anxiety from when she was first born is surging. I've been obsessing lately about my breastfeeding mistakes. How she would have been much happier if I would have just nursed her more, but my stubbornness really got in the way. Was remembering that paralyzed feeling of not being able to go anywhere or do anything because of her naps and feedings. I just couldn't get it together. It's been flooding back lately. I guess because it's getting close to A coming home. I'm afraid that I'm not good enough for him.

As a wife, friend, partner, mom of the family. I'm really dog tired. The kind of tired that caffeine has no effect on.

June 11, 2017

Tears fall in between passing strangers on the street. Sometimes I'm so sad, I just let them flow no matter where I am: at the grocery store or the drug store, in the parking lot while she sleeps in the car seat. I've spent so many hours waiting in parking lots for her to finish her nap. Don't dare touch her or she wakes up. These naps are the precious quiet times I am so desperate for.

June 12, 2017

She brought my socks to me in the afternoon because she wanted to go out. It is so hot. We walked around the neighborhood a little, stopping for a mango popsicle at the local Cinco de Mayo grocery store. Sat in the grass at the church across the street from our house, our front yard. The popsicle was all over her face, dripping down her chin, happy as a clam. Perfect summer moment.

OPTING IN

I MUST NOT BE afraid. I must press on. I must live with a fierce love in my heart.

I am powerless over tragedy, death, and violence. I am also powerless over the most beautiful things life has to offer: a golden setting sun, new snow, swirling stars. As I watch a sunrise in the city, over crumbling row houses and sidewalks strewn with trash, I see the beauty that can't be held back. The twinkle of a crescent moon, a soft orange overtaking a waning blue sky.

They can't be stopped, the sun and moon and stars. Neither can love. Humanity is made of love, and nothing we do can stop that.

My job today is to burn bright with love, hope, and faith. I cannot change the beauty of humanity any more than I can turn the tides of the ocean or fight the waves. I cannot change that I have been given everything I need in this moment.

I cannot stop the glorious sun from rising in the east.

CONTENTMENT

I WAS STEADILY WALKING a path toward a shiny city, a good place to rest. I was getting close. The path took a slight right turn toward some pastures. I thought it may be the scenic route. But the path kept angling farther and farther away, down a softly sloping mountain, through the countryside and into a dark wood. The city well behind me by now. Far, far away.

The long journey finally came to a close. I've made it home, made it full circle, the city a distant mirage. My girl led me all the way with her golden ribbon. Now I must be reborn, renewed, risen. Fear has died, faith has triumphed. This is a new beginning with no tracks behind.

I've never found deep contentment in anything but raising her. It's a challenge that comes with a sensation of absolutely no regrets. I would do it all again, to have this child and to be able to kiss her forehead.

GOD

God is a clear pool of water.

God is the ocean waves, a waterfall, a trickling
  stream.

God is rain, snow, bathwater, a cold glass of water.

God is the foundation of my coffee, a dirty
  puddle in the alley, the steam rising from the
  concrete.

God is 60% me.

SELF-LOVE

DEAR GWEN,

Today I want to greet you with the message that, yes, this is enough. This is enough because this is it. This is what you get, you on a plate.

It never gets easy. Ella will grow up, you will get old, you will have several dogs, houses, cars, jobs, degrees, failures, and successes. That anxious, fearful pit in your stomach never goes away because that's what keeps you going. You will one day discover that you have lived a daring and incredibly adventurous life. You will unfortunately never consider it enough, but that's because you are very brave. You long for simplicity, yet you strive to compact your life with adventure after adventure. This will be your lifelong push–pull. This is part of who you are. It is ok.

Look at your hands right now. What are they doing? Mine are holding a baby in one and marking this page with a pen in the other. Sometimes, you may need to wash your hands and start clean. But most times, you need to just look at what they are holding.

Now listen, this is important. Whatever is in those hands right now, treat it as if it is precious. Gold precious, diamond precious, newborn baby precious. You were given such things without having to be perfect. Such things are not a reward for good behavior. You have what you hold because you are loved. You are enough.

And I promise, even those times when all you hold is a microwave burrito and your last crumpled dollar, you are loved. Someone's got your back. Someone died for you.

I've given up lots of times, convinced myself it is not to be. I've shuttered the windows on my dreams over and over and over. But that dang light, the desire, won't get put out, it still seeps through the cracks, still glows behind the closed window.

Dreams never go away. Dreams never leave us.

I might feel silly. I might be low. I might be try-ing to hide my dreamy self under layers of respon-sibility and laziness and fear. I may have given up a few times, but dreams never go away.

Just give it a chance. Listen to the still small something, that tiny voice. That heartbeat. It may not bring me fame. It may not bring wealth. But it might bring love, joy, or something closer to faith. It's very likely that in this lifetime there will be no extrinsic reward for listening to this dream, for letting this light through the window warm your face. I don't know that following this dream will ever lead anywhere.

What I do know is that these dreams, they will never leave you alone.

So keep going, will you? Light the candle of divine inspiration. Hold the flame close and write. Keep writing. She will sleep by your side, loved, nurtured, and cared for. You have a job to do. It's time. Keep taking risks and embrace the fear you feel. But, take breaks when you need to. Have fun. Pick flowers. Let go.

Love,
Gwen

THE BETWIXT

Stopping for a quick hike on the Appalachian Trail, a place where I can commune with a sense of pilgrimage close to home, it isn't long before the quiet crunch of winter leaves and the other worldly pallet of mosses bring me into the betwixt. I gain momentum by simply walking forward, walking along a path, and allowing my shoulders to drop and my mind to open. It is a place between reality and the imagined. At once both real and dream, and also neither reality nor imagination. In the betwixt, I am free.

. . .

The betwixt is the absolute most delicious place to be. Here, there is magic, ideas, God. Here, there are no rules, time, or expectations. I am able to enter the betwixt most successfully in nature, alone, without distractions. I am also able to enter with pen in hand, alone, without distractions. As a matter of fact, just by you reading this, we have both entered, together. I am not always able to enter when I try to, therefore making the betwixt a very hard place to reach indeed. Portals to this liminal space include:

- nature
- hiking
- writing
- coffee
- sunrise
- sunset
- baking
- stars
- water
- trees
- sweeping quiet

It can be scary at first, leaving reality behind without the comfort of knowing it's a daydream. There are all sorts of noises from other beings and sometimes shadows or whispers. It is hard to know if I have gone crazy or if this is just the weirdness of creativity, like this book, a mix of real-life events, wishes, and magic.

When I am in reality, without my imagination, I buzz with anxiety and fear. I do not trust that things will work out. When I am in daydream land, I neglect adventure and lack experiences. When nothing happens outside your dream, well, nothing happens. Dreams are really nice, and dreams are helpful, but they don't cross over into reality without a lot of coaxing.

But in the betwixt, I can be everything I dream of. I can allow magic to sparkle and glow. I can see that the real is not real and the not real is real. The trick is figuring out how to enter that place. The real trick is staying there.

· · ·

The highway back into view, I step slowly down the last of the trail, passing under a Civil War era stone arch and back into reality. My mind is suddenly crammed with memories and ideas, with hope. All the footsteps that have collected on that trail, infused with the promise of the through-hiker, have leaked into the soles of my boots.

LETTING WISHES IN

Fairies. Angels. Animal messengers. Sunsets. Waterfalls. A mysterious glen. Moss-covered trees. A gurgling creek. A cozy yellow house on the edge of a wood. Firelight. Stew in a pot. Stories after midnight. Hiking trails. Deer in the yard. A million stars. A sleeping dog. A cold night. Quilts. Hot tea with honey. Cinnamon on the stove. A worn, wooden table. A comfy reading chair. Snow in winter. Long summer days. A dirty picture window. Front porch swing. A trampoline. Dusty tennis shoes. Lightning bugs in a jar. Pie crust. A peach tree. Bicycles at dusk. An old friend. Laughter. Tears. Card games. Poetry. Bible verses. A map of the world. A big adventure.

IMAGINATION

We go hiking, you and I, to check on our fairies. I ask if you think they've been there, and you answer absolutely yes. I believe you. I believe in you.

Just off our regular path, you find a fairy tunnel buried under a tree, hidden by some tall grass. Today, we place some items for the fairies inside: an eggshell, some pieces of glass, a bluish feather, and real snake skin. You rearrange our set of fairy dishes made from shells, stones, and acorns, the bed made from branches and leaves, and some pretty beads in a tiny wooden box, and cover up the door carefully with a piece of bark, making sure it is camouflaged.

Just beyond the nearby creek is a clearing with some tall grass and mushrooms. Sunshine has filled the clearing, and the mushrooms are very large and orange. We sit on an old log, and you look carefully for special moss or twigs that the fairies could use.

An owl descends from the sky and lands on a log opposite to us. We acknowledge him. He peers at the mushrooms too, tilting his head. We all wait for something to happen. A caterpillar makes his way over my barefoot. You laugh a twinkling laugh and keep searching under the log for fairy dishes. Little droplets of water sparkle on the grass.

We eventually walk out of the betwixt and back to the house. Pancakes are kept warm in the oven, and coffee steams in a percolator on the stove. Dad greets you with a squeeze and rubs your nose with his cheeks. We sit at our smooth wooden dining table as I slide a window open to let air move through the screen. The radio chatters the day's news as we pile our pancakes with freshly cut peaches. Us three laugh about something only we think is funny and feed the old dog scraps from the table.

After breakfast, I retire to my spot on the front porch to write, watching you ride your bike up and down the long driveway. Later, we tend to the garden while Dad makes some lemonade for porch swinging. Our neighbors drop by with huge, green tomatoes which we trade for flowers, some greens, and a jar of peaches in brandy.

TIMELESSNESS

Ella and I are sitting on the shore of Timothy Lake. She is about four and I am about ten. We both have ponytails, and it's the end of the day. Our bare feet play with the round stones that make up the lake floor. The sky is a solid glow of burnt orange. We have a fairy boat ready to set sail. The candle is lit, and she wonders without asking what I will wish for. Creativity of course. Inspiration. The candle goes out, and Ella laughs.

I wake with her head on my chest. I nestle my nose in her hair, and she squiggles closer to me in her sleep.

This time we are floating in the lake, cheek to cheek. The sky still completely orange, reflected in the water, we breathe in orange and cream. The water is warm and enveloping. She is four, but she is also much older.

I wake again. She slumps over, off of my chest to lay

on her tummy.

We are now under a starry sky, swirling with galaxies.

I wake up. She is still asleep.

It is finally sunrise, bright orange and pink. Someone is making the hot chocolate. Someone is stoking the fire; a few coals still burn from the night before.

FREEDOM
(*required)

I NEVER DID CARRY any of the heavy things alone. My God held my hand as I walked, my hair as I puked. He lifted me up when I fell, cooled my forehead when seething with rage, paved the way when I was blindfolded. My God never left me, never will leave me, and loves me for being the true imperfect me.

I'm waiting for you, lonely, pain-soaked traveler. I've been there, too. I've got a warm meal and clean sheets and hugs. You are welcome here, friend. This house is yours. The road is yours, too. Go on and find your freedom, no need to pack light. But do be sure to bring:

- Honesty*
- Courage*

- The willingness to free fall*—don't just stand on the edge, jump off of it, there might not be a net but jump anyway.
- Trust*—in God, in the abyss, in cigarettes, in something.

APPRECIATION

Six months or so after my daughter was born, I sat in a posh coffee shop in downtown Baltimore writing in a journal and sipping a cappuccino. There was a man seated at a table nearby who smiled in my direction several times. He was about my father's age, with a late 60s overcoat and glasses. He packed his things into a very old leather accordion briefcase. As he passed my table, he smiled again and asked, "Do you ever read them?"

"Read what?" I replied, amused.

"Your journals," he answered. "I journal every day and love to go back and read them."

"Oh no, no, no," I exclaimed. "I never read them. I keep them, but never go back."

"Ah! You must!" he said earnestly. "You need to read them." And then he set in on telling me his writing accomplishments at length, leaving me with a copy of an article he published in the local paper in the mid-90s. We happened to live in the same neighborhood. I gave him my card, and we vowed to meet for coffee sometime.

Of course, I never saw him again. He was a messenger when I needed a message. It was because of him that, upon going back and sifting through a pile of journals from the past few years, I realized this book had already been written. All I needed to do was decipher my own handwriting and put it in an order that made some sense. So thank you, Mr. Coffee Shop Angel Man, for delivering that message.

• • •

If I could summarize my early 30s in just one word, that word would be humbling. I used to be a really great speaker, had no problem getting up in front of a room full of people. In those days, I knew everything about all things. Now I'm faced with the distinct realization that I know absolutely nothing. And I'm okay with it.

I wrote this because I have always wanted to write, to be a writer, and I believe we should do the things we really want to do, even if we are not the best at that thing. I also wrote this because, although

I know next to nothing, I believe that collectively, as people, we know things. If I add my voice and my experience to the pot of millions of other voices and experiences, then maybe, together, we can know things. Maybe we can teach each other and grow and make less mistakes or maybe even be willing to make more of them.

Thank you, Marie, Rachael and Cija, for sifting through the early drafts. Thank you Kapua for nudging this project along; you are so patient. Thank you A, for believing in me, no questions asked. Thank you, Ella, for inspiring me tell your story, too.

This is my story. Thank you for letting me share my voice. We are all in this together.

ABOUT THE AUTHOR

Gwen Van Velsor writes creative nonfiction and pseudo-inspirational prose. She has written for Baltimore Style, Huffington Post, Summit Daily, and Big Island Chronicle, among other publications. Raised in Portland, Oregon, Gwen has moved many times, from sea to shining sea, now calling Highlandtown, Baltimore her forever home. Her major accomplishments include walking the Camino de Santiago pilgrimage in Spain, raising a toddler, and being okay with life exactly as it is. Her memoir, *Follow That Arrow*, was published in 2016.

YELLOW ARROW

PUBLISHING

Thank you for supporting independent publishing.
The mission of Yellow Arrow is to support women
writers through publication and access to the
literary arts.

For more information on our non-profit work or
to order the hand-bound companion journal to
Freedom Warrior, visit
YellowArrowPublishing.com